Captured Moments

Selected Poems

By Ellenelizabeth Cernek

ISBN 978-1-936373-19-2

© 2011 Ellenelizabeth Cernek. All rights reserved. No part of this publication may be reproduced or transmitted in any form or by any means, electronic or mechanical, without permission in writing from the publisher. Requests for permission to make copies of any part of this work should be e-mailed to info@unboundcontent.com.

Published in the United States by Unbound Content, LLC, Englewood, NJ.

Cover art: Autumn Mums ©2008, by Ellenelizabeth Cernek-Kashk.

Author photo: John James Schwartz

The poems in this collection are all original and previously unpublished with the exception of those credited otherwise.

Captured Moments

First edition 2011

Dedication

I would like to thank my muse, who has been in my life since I was 11. The torrid love affair we have had over many years has fueled my poetry with passion, lust, love, longing, sorrow, and fun. He is my lover and best friend for more than 40 years and there hasn't been a day that he has not made me smile.

—Ellenelizabeth Cernek

Table of Contents

Introduction 9

Contemplating Composition

Take My Hand 13
Directions 14
Soaring Deep 15
Poetry in the Garden 16

Sometimes Things Scatter

Be As 19
Beach Reverie 20
Trails of Tales 22
A Minute Kink 24
Empty Space 25

Love or Something Like It

Footprints of a Wildfire 29
Sun Worship 30
Harbor of Love 32
Peaceful Rhythm 34
Close Your Eyes 35
Madison Bridges 36
Exhilarate 37
The Eternity 38

It All Hangs on a Question

To Remember 41
Fire That Echoes 42
Vagabond 43
Obscure Passing of Echoing Time 44
Mangoes 46
Wholesome? 47
Rabbits & Death 48

Crossroads 49
Backwash 50
Autumn's Waltz 51

Domesticities

Cocoon 55
Hunting 56
Within Its Own Cage 58
Upon the Window 59
Roof Deck 60
My Silent Corner 62
Where 64

Far-Flung Corners of the World

330 Square Meters 69
My Alexandria 70
The Blue Hole 72
Location 74
Inky Nights 75
Sinai Traveler 76
Unobtainable? 78
Mersa Matruh 80
My Heart Beckons 81
Sophie's Window 82
The Faces It Touches 84
Gypsy Road 85

Magic Alive

Hunter Mountain 89
Watchwoman 90
Shahenda 92
Creation of Shahenda 94
Shahenda's Vocation 96
Blue 98
Path's End 100

About the Author 103

Captured Moments

Introduction

What classifies a work as romance poetry? To some degree, the same things that classify certain works of fiction as romance novels: a sense of adventure, exotic locale, hardships unexpected and hardships overcome. And always, always, always, a pervasive awareness of love, the poetic language of love imbued with tones mystical, cerebral, physical, and historical.

The poetry of Ellenelizabeth Cernek definitely falls into the category of romance poetry. You'll know it from first read, just like we sometimes know love at first sight. So what does one do to prepare for a romance poetry read? The same things you'd do to prepare for any flight of fancy or spectacular vacation. Open your heart and mind to the adventure that awaits. Pack light; you don't want to be bogged down. You never know what remote reaches are right around the turn of the next page. The journey begins at a desk, continues to a roof deck, to a beach, extends all over the world to places such as Hunter Mountain, NY, and Alexandria, Egypt, and even takes us through the constellations so that we can whisper with the moon.

When you're ready, turn the page and take Ellenelizabeth up on her invitation:

Take my hand, let us embark
Through captured moments
Of my heart

As hand in hand
*   We start*

Annmarie Lockhart
Fall 2011

Contemplating Composition

Captured Moments

Take My Hand

Echo of a long since forgotten time
Begs to become a rhyme.
Take my hand; I'll escort you through
To explore the world
Which I once knew.

Take my hand; I'll glide with you
To places, and among their people who,
Have cluttered my mind's heart.

Take my hand, you'll see through my eyes
The experiences and maybe some lies,
From where I've said many good-byes.

Take my hand, let us embark,
Through captured moments,
Of my heart

As hand in hand
        We start.

Ellenelizabeth Cernek

Directions

As if the howling wind
Knew of my only sin.
As if the dark night
Knew of my only plight.
As if the cold morning air
Knew of my longing to share.

My emotions are rare,
Causing my ability to share,
To bellow from deep within my heart,
Wishing our togetherness never to part.

    And it seems to me
    As if you knew,
    The next direction
    The wind blew.

First appeared in Rhyme and Reason, *1996.*

Captured Moments

Soaring Deep

Within seas — Within seas
Silent, with a quiet
Frightened attitude.
Alone, with an increased need for sharing,
Unsure, with an obsession
Of the man-made guilt.
Blurs of emotions,
Rushing throughout my body.
My spirit has been set free to fly,
On a journey through
Lapses within lapses of extended time.
Forever going — Never ending.
Blurs of emotions and
Rushes of energy,
Bursts of sharing.
Simultaneous experiences
Of being,
Exploring,
Extending,
Acknowledging the atmosphere,
And the presence of this energy.
Capable of showing the inner being
And never knowing the man-made guilt.
Energy flying,
Soaring deep within
Seas within seas

First appeared in Treasured Poems of America, *Fall 1996.*

Ellenelizabeth Cernek

Poetry in the Garden

Reading from all the masters
Discussing their true intent
Within the afternoon's blaze of sunshine.

Like entering a forgotten garden,
Lost within the clutter of a busy town
Enchanted with its hues of green.

The ivy encircled a fallen snake-like tree.
Upon the center stump, naturally sculpted
A piece of driftwood stood gracefully as sentry.

Ah! The symmetry of greenery that
One observes while gliding upon
The garden's thin footpaths;
Causing the soul to hush and quiet.

On the porch, the masters spoke
Through the gardener's characteristic voice.

To calm the soul
To speak and pierce the heart
To listen and learn the silence,

As her garden grows.

Sometimes Things Scatter

Captured Moments

Be As

Where feelings engulf
With massive kinetic energy
There are we to be found.

Where the inner tides
Flow through our veins
There are we, on our journey

Where amber shades of gold
Fill our cups
There are we, overflowing.

Where indifference and bewilderment
Flare into peace,
There are we, finding inner utopia.

Where our companionship and sharing
Cause our love to flourish
There are we,

Joined as one.

Ellenelizabeth Cernek

Beach Reverie

Did you ever sit on the beach
On a cold, cloudy, drizzly day?
Looking out on the icy blue ocean ...
How fierce and uncontrollable it is!
How its waves grow strong as monsters,
To end up crashing upon the shore!

Did you ever think of the reason "Why"?
Old fishermen say: "It's Neptune's fury
Punishing some sailor on the high seas."
They are old superstitious men
Frightened of the unknown.
Scholarly men give logical reasons,
Having to do with the winds
Or the moon pulling the earth,
Causing tides ....

Yet today I gaze upon the ocean,
A haunting feeling comes over me
The sun in my hair, on my face ...
I walk with him once again,
I hear his laughter,
As we run in the sand.

Captured Moments

With joy and tranquility
I remember love shared
In my yester-years ...

Then a brisk wind wakes me,
From my beach reverie.

I turn and walk away
To find comfort
In the warmth of the bungalow.
Smiling, for there too
Are wonderful memories,
Of my father.

Trails of Tales

    As you meet
Eyes gaze then shy away
    As you learn
Questions are asked
But where is the truth?
    As you love
A trust is to be gained ...
    As you hear
Stories become trails of tales
    As you cry
Eyes glare, swell, and tear
    Truth and trust of your love
Give way to questions
Answered by trails of tales
    As you try to believe
Holding onto what may be left
Of the life you thought you'd built
    As you listen
Oceans and seas roar and soar
You just hear the lapping away upon the shores

Captured Moments

    As you feel
Your heart tearing and voices screeching
    As your life of
Happily ever after
Is being torn out of your
Favorite fairy tale
With the trails of tales
Which are only lies.

Ellenelizabeth Cernek

A Minute Kink

Somehow within the searching
I happened upon a minute kink
Within the steeled armor.

As I was absorbed in
I rushed
To find the soul.

As I touched this soul
I learned to crawl,
To walk, to soar.

As I fell into this deep,
Cold, voided heart
Within his steeled armor,
I found a flicker
Of love still alive.
As it ignited
The fires of desire flared
Passion roared and soared.

And love still lives
Under the steeled armor
Where I happened upon
A minute kink
Which ignited a lost soul.

Captured Moments

Empty Space

In silence I place my left hand open
Upon the clean cold pane of glass.
It is my left hand that feels the cold,
Which travels to the empty space within my heart.

In remembrance of the illusion I believed in
In remembrance of the lost and found friendship,
In remembrance of the careless days, and wishful nights.

In silence I place my left hand open
Upon the clean cold pane of glass.
It is my remembrance, which is all I hold of the past,
Which travels to the empty space within my heart.

Love or Something Like It

Captured Moments

Footprints of a Wildfire

I will taunt you
So you will follow

I will caress you
'Til you are consumed

I will love you
Leaving only embers

I will die for you
Extinguishing the
Footprints of my wildfire

First appeared at: http://www.aquillrelle.com/magpoetrymishmash.htm#p6.

Sun Worship

      On a hot tar roof, in mid-morn,
I silently lay spread eagle.
      As afternoon unveils hot rays,
Which caress my naked body,
I am conscious of his presence.
      His rays of light are absorbed
Deep within me, exciting me.
Yet he has not touched me,
He is just growing nearer,
Caressing every inch of my nakedness
Within his warming glow.
      I can feel my excitement growing,
As his light penetrates my skin.
Gently fondling my every aspect of being
Causing sweat to blossom at my nape.
      Gently I roll, deep within desires being fulfilled,
As he stands there watching.

Captured Moments

      Lying on my stomach,
I feel his heat massaging my back,
And flowing to my buttocks,
Setting my entire body afire.
      Relaxing after the ecstasy,
I fall into a light slumber.
Holding fast and dreaming of his warmth and excitement.
      Awakened quite suddenly, by a cold breeze blowing,
He is gone behind a cloud.
      In my not-yet-shaken-off slumber, I do wonder ...
If tomorrow I may enjoy
The light and warmth of his presence,
Or will my day be cloudy and gray, with no sun bathing.

First appeared at Wings, *Vol 7 No 1, Fall 1997.*

Harbor of Love

I leave the black wrought-iron gate ajar
My signal to you, if you ride by
To bring the sweetness of your love
Into the warmth of my waiting heart.
In the silence of early morn,
      You come to me,
Bring raw passion,
The longing desire,
The fire in lust
Of our eternal love.
We embrace, as if years
Have passed since our last encounter
Yet it was only hours since we touched.
Our lovemaking begins slowly, gently
Each counteracting the other's motions,
Our animal needs enhancing and intensifying
As our motions quicken.
Clawing and biting each other with unquenchable desires
We collide and expel against one another.
You cause me to forget to breathe
As I drown in our love.

Captured Moments

You spread my arms cross like
Pinning me down, as your rhythm is a constant flow
Making the world stop.
We roll; you hold my breasts, then glide to my hips
Always keeping our movements synchronized,
Exactly hitting my internal itch.
You pull at my hair as I reach one of many peaks.
Moving together with groans, heavy breathing, and sweet sweat
We conclude in a shared climax
And tumble against the bed
Intertwined, satisfied, content.
We doze off within the harbor of each other's arms
Knowing the outside world cannot touch us.

Peaceful Rhythm

I glide my nose against
Your temple
Gently kissing your cheek
I inhale deeply
Drinking in your scent
We lay in the late afternoon
On a camouflage blanket
The haze of the day
Burning our skin
Salt air blows gently
Rustling your chest hairs
You slip off into sleep
I know you've been working
Long and strange hours
So I watch the inhale
And exhale of your breath
Synchronizing with the lapping waves
Becoming a peaceful rhythm

Captured Moments

Close Your Eyes

Close your eyes
As I grasp your hand
Gently turning
Your wrist skyward

Softly I brush
My lower lip against
The inner part of
Your wrist
I look up at you
As you quiver
I giggle at the
Barometer I have
On and with you
I gently suck
Feeling your pulse
Dracula like

I close my eyes
Feel the heat of
Your pulse
Deep within my body
Exciting me

I open my eyes
I am on the morning bus
Only thinking of you

Ellenelizabeth Cernek

Madison Bridges
(Inspired by The Bridges of Madison County, the movie)

The movie stirred my heart
About a love that had to part
Knowing of the fight
Only silences the night
The forbidden love
Unleashed the hidden dove
Enabling it to take flight
Within the quiet memories of plight
Knowing that it is right to part
Keeping its memories within the heart
Until their deaths
       Free their souls
              Nevermore to part

Captured Moments

Exhilarate

Things have burned,
      A fire has been set.
Echoes of what could have been
      Interpreted, miscommunicated.
The here and now reminds me
      Of a love that once was
Stirring lost love,
      Igniting desires
Holding one, to stolen moments
      Of a past
That belonged to bad timing
      Of the could-bes
           Would-bes
      Of my happiness.

I breathe you in,
      As you exhilarate me.

Ellenelizabeth Cernek

The Eternity

Within your hands
I cautiously place again
My heart

Hold it gently
Protect it from the
Rains, winds, and storms
Which may come

Speak your heart to mine
So I can listen
And feel our love
As our hearts beat together
For eternity

The eternity
I've been waiting
And searching for

It All Hangs on a Question

Captured Moments

To Remember

for all the lost dreams
for all the misbegotten
> Could-bes
> Should-bes
> Would-bes

and
> What-ifs

are always within the wind's
echo of the past

the misbegottens
> never to be forgotten

always to be remembered

for all the lost dreams
for all the misbegottens
> Could-bes
> Should-bes
> Would-bes

and
> What-ifs
> of life

it is only
> to remember

Ellenelizabeth Cernek

Fire That Echoes

Within the silence of a foggy brain
Colors burst out of the blackness
Within the shadows of the iridescent words
Echoes the glance of fire
Silver pours like teardrops
Yet never will it douse
The glances and chances
Of the fire that echoes
Within the silence of a foggy brain
    As you drive by

Captured Moments

Vagabond

What river do you see in me?
For I am only but a tree,
Standing upon the riverbanks,
For shade is all my thanks.

To spread my arms open wide,
For the foolish child's game of hide.

What river do you see within me?
For I am only but the tree
Guarding the riverbanks,
To aid a child with some pranks.

To stand and watch the river flow
Under root and trunk, allowing me to grow.

What river do you see
Me upon? For only the fallen tree,
Is a vagabond.

Ellenelizabeth Cernek

Obscure Passing of Echoing Time

As white rivers quietly
Rush in tandem
Abandoned in a time forgotten
Captured in the sins of the mother
Forever disconnected
In the echoing time
Of then, of now?

As I look into the blue gray sky
When the pinks and mauves
Of sunset have faded
And the darkness
Has yet to arrive
Staring up past the blue spruces
Which have been here before me
And I shall leave before them

The topmost branches
Still defined before
Darkness swallows the
Last breath of daylight

Captured Moments

High above tiny white and red
Lights blink
A jet passes with no sound
Darkness breathes
Covering the world

I am disconnected
As I witness the birthing
Of the first evening star

Echoing to me
The obscure passing of time

First appeared at: http://www.angelfire.com/mo/dot/obscure.html.

Ellenelizabeth Cernek

Mangoes

Where did God place the first mango?
Did it come from the mythical garden of Paradise?

Was it green skinned, with luscious, sweet orange pulp
As found in Egypt?

Or was it pale orange skinned, with vibrant orange souls
As found in Mexico?

How many mangoes did Adam and Eve eat?
How many kinds were in the garden of Paradise?
Did they eat them all?

Before she got into
        What kind of apple?

Wholesome?

Listen to the chanted whispers of the Goddess
Where the essential drool is worshipping.
That inner fluff, to describe a picture
Of the delirious visions the mind remembers
Hearing the forest's languished dreams
Among winter's shadows,
The fall's leaves,
Throughout summer's light,
And the spring's mist,
      Describing the remembrance
           Of thoughts that cause pleasure.

Ellenelizabeth Cernek

Rabbits & Death

I came across an emerald green field
And happened to fall into a hole
Where Alice's rabbit bit my ass
So I had to chase him through
This illuminating tunnel
Where the one-eyed Jack,
Kissed the black Ace of Spades
And caused the sentence of disgrace
The court was held in that same field
Where I had fallen
        In love with a Black Ace
And found myself sentenced
                To a living death.

Captured Moments

Crossroads

Life again and again
Finds only crossroads
Where now and before
Shall turn into a tomorrow.

Worry not in this
Crossroad's time
For this will always
Pass into a yesterday.

Life again and again
Finds only crossroads,
Where life will again
Be always new.

Ellenelizabeth Cernek

Backwash

The backwash of the Atlantic waves
Spills over my size ten foot.
Hunched over, gazing upon
The gifts the wave carries in
I walk along the beach
In silent contemplation
Collecting the treasures,
The ocean's discards.
Peace and tranquility are the sounds
Cooing and caressing the shore.
The ocean's natural gifts given freely,
As the backwash of the Atlantic waves
Spills over my size ten foot
And silently cleanses my soul.

Captured Moments

Autumn's Waltz

The mirror answers, my flower
Monsters together forget,
Summer flies easily by:
Over blue mountains,
Around white castle clouds,
Under green lake pools,
Traveling slowly higher
Turning light wings of love,
      Pink.

As we pulled down the pumpkin moon,
The gardener's beds cocoon,
      Into fall:
Starting leaves to dance and twirl.

Domesticities

Captured Moments

Cocoon

She is stuck
Within a cocoon
Her beauty needs now
To see the moon.

One life to lead
As she completes
Nature's cruel cycle.

Webbed always in
The knowing of desire ...

Life leads
As her deed is done.

Trapped within her cocoon.

Hunting

Tethered to an apartment
A home uncertain
Of position
In family
In friendship
In work
In worth

Tethered to the land
Falling stone
Falling water
Churning
Turning
In change

Tethered to people
In uncomfortable control
With him
With them
With us
In me

Captured Moments

Tethered to
Inconsolable winds
I am riding high
Searching
Family
Friends
Him
Us
Them
Hunting for me

Ellenelizabeth Cernek

Within Its Own Cage

I hate seeing anything caged.
Yet alone within
My mahogany and linens
I am to be.

When in need of affection
I may watch
My curtains shiver
And move to the rhythm of
The ceiling fan.

Or listen to my lovebirds
Locked within their home
Ralph and Alice continuing quibbles.

Where is the affection
In our life's day to day?
When neither can read the other
For each is locked

Within its own cage.

Captured Moments

Upon the Window

My nightly view of condensation
Sweating down the window
Dishes piled like
A skyscraper
Within the double sink
Rubber gloved hands
To protect the sensitive skin

Steam rises
Sweat upon the brow
Always staring at the view
Of condensation beading
Upon the window.

Ellenelizabeth Cernek

Roof Deck

Dawn pushes away the empty blackness
To dance on the pink, yellow, blue-gray houses
Of the neighbors
Their vinyl glistening of morning dew
The mourning doves
Coo on top of air conditioners
Sparrows chirping
Their mating rituals as they fly from
Rooftop to gutters
My moist backyard dirt
Robins look for worms
The big brown cauldron-looking planter
Is coming alive with strawberries
I am allergic to them
I grow them for John
The lilies have started
Their ascent from the urn
I planted them last year
The steel 3-foot trough-like planter
My herbs
Early morning on my roof deck
My oasis

Captured Moments

Then the cars start going by
The train in the meadow toots
7:00 am everyone up
The 100-year-old house groans
The dogs need letting out
A crane flies west overhead
Somewhere for the East or Hudson rivers
To the Meadowlands, Hackensack River
Time to make the coffee

First appeared at: http://issuu.com/pigeonbike/docs/pb_and_coffee.

Ellenelizabeth Cernek

My Silent Corner

Mish-Mish peacefully purrs
Curly pants heavily
The air is hot and thick
Do-Do is trying to sleep
      And I, in my maroon and white corner
Silently weeping
Pulling the soul from
Whatever I have left of the body
The mind begs for sleep
And races simultaneously
The night summer's air is heavy
As so is my heart
I wish for just a slight breeze
To cool me
Yet it is not coming
The snowflake window is open
A car goes by
Somewhere in the distance
Voices are heard, but not understood
Maybe they aren't talking
It's the dead air carrying
Some lost thought in the dark night
A thought which has fallen
Upon a deaf world

Captured Moments

My own words, feelings of despair
Of what tomorrow shall bring
Keep falling upon the misunderstood world
Around me
Pen in hand releases all …
Mish-Mish stirs, questioning
My tear-swept green eyes, swishes his tail
And jaunts away, Curly still pants
From this airless summer's night heat
Oh Storm! Come, clean all!
My heart is so heavy
A boom of fireworks over the Hudson or East rivers
Echoes up the cliff, to my snowflake window
I can almost see the blaze of colors
Within my thought-filled mind
Or is it the thunderstorm
That is to come?

Ellenelizabeth Cernek

Where

I've been having this dream

Where your arms spread open,
Beckoning me into your embrace.

Where your hands cup my chin,
Raise my face to meet yours.

Where you gently lift the shroud off
My shoulders giving me peace within your warmth.

Where the sea air breathes freshness
And cleanses my senses alive once more.

Where the mountain dew dances lightly
On my naked skin in a cool dawn
Forgiving all my faults.

Where the afternoon's bright rays capture
All the brilliance of your smile on me.

Captured Moments

Where the illuminating full moon on a lake
Pales in your presence as you glide across the waters.

Where in the thickness of a fog
You are the beacon of light
Guiding my way back home.

Where finally I can see your face
As I see my own reflection

Clear and not distorted by dreams.

Where are you now?

Far-Flung Corners of the World

Captured Moments

330 Square Meters

I hear
        Earth calling
The sandy white dust
        Speaks like an angel
Asking for my return home

I hear
        Sea calling
The salty blue waves
        Speak like an omen
Asking for my presence within

I hear
        Desert road calling
As African sun blisters upon the flatness
        Speaks like a lonely soul
Asking for my being

I hear
        Heat calling
The brilliant blaze upon the cliffs
        Speaks like photos in an album
Asking for my heart

The earth, by the sea, upon the cliffs
        Keeps echoing to the soul
Asking where I've been

Ellenelizabeth Cernek

My Alexandria
(Egypt, August 1997)

Awakened by the early morning call to prayer
Men and women bow in homage to God,
Breaking the night's slumber.
Within close range the rattling tan and blue tram
Seen and heard screeching to the stop below.
Upon the seventh-floor balcony,
Peering below as the world awakens
Coming alive with sights and sounds.
Horses or donkeys laden with carts,
Filled to capacity with market goods,
Proceeding steadily upon the hot tar,
A breath of sea air now and again
Revives the overburdened beasts.
A big blue truck filled with boxes of fresh fish
Caught before dawn,
Passes quickly below to the market.
Yellow/black or orange/black taxis
In unending motion and sound,
Zoom over the tram's tracks
In and about each other,
Always squealing horns
For each are sounding off their own tunes.

Captured Moments

The ching ching of the lonely juice man passes below.
These are the sounds that greet me
Early morning,
In my Alexandria

Ellenelizabeth Cernek

The Blue Hole
(Dahab, Sinai, Egypt, August 1997)

Step carefully with *ship-ship*, sandals or water shoes,
The water-washed rocks are round
On which you place your feet.
Enter the *mia* (water) with care and curiosity,
Mask and snorkel in hand.

Step lightly for all is alive beneath your feet.
Walk the hundred yards to the edge
Of the continental shelf.
Place mask upon face: insert snorkel within mouth,
Glide above the massive shelf.

The Red Sea is heavy laden in salt,
Making one buoyant, as if flying above.
Open your eyes and peer upon
Bushes of coral coloring the shelf's walls,
In blues, pinks, greens, and whites,
Each its own colony of marine life.

Swim with the blue, black, and silver fish
Close enough to touch.
See the hand of God grace the water
As rays of silver white light dance
Before you within the aqua blue sea.

Captured Moments

Swim among the coins of transparent fish
Sprinkled before you.
Spy upon the colored corals
Coming alive with their own colored fish.

Watch the fluorescent green fish
With ruby-lipped smile,
Move his big yellow eye up to see
What fish you are.

Amazing the cast of color
Within the marine life
God has placed
Around the blue hole.

Ellenelizabeth Cernek

Location

Where is the graffiti
Written across time
To mark your location
Forever in time

Symbols, pictographs, hieroglyphs
Primitive cave drawings, crop drawings
Diagrams, illustrations
Cartoons, doodles
Creating and engaging imaginations
Of what is trying to be said

In an old Roman town
The African town of Timgad
Graffiti was found
It said:

Hunting, bathing
Playing, laughing
That is what life is about!

Written across time
To mark a location
Thousands of years ago

Location, location, location
To place graffiti for the future
Marking your forever in time
What would you say?

Captured Moments

Inky Nights

I've danced on Mt. Sinai
Under the ink black night
Cursing the dawn
And fearing being alone
For I am not the true
Sunlight
Just an illusion
A spirit in flight
Romancing my passion
And dancing with pen
All I have are memories
Of the last dance
In the inky night
Dancing in my mind
Of Mt. Sinai
And you

Ellenelizabeth Cernek

Sinai Traveler

Wisps of desert grass blow
Along the straits of the road
The bald rock mountains
Baked and eroded in a time forgotten
Rise and fall as the traveler
Marvels through the mini-bus window.
A camel sits and chews in the heat of the day
Beside a Bedouin campsite
Multicolored tents are scattered
Around the snippet of greenery
That the desert allows living
The road begins to turn and turn
Around the bald mountains
A giant turtle-shaped rock
Sits among the white sands of a valley
In his thousandth year of silent meditation
Sand blasted mountains, made jagged
With wind, baked by sun, eroded with storm
Lie alongside the turtle, and the road ahead.
Browns, whites, grays of the Sinai Desert
Are only interrupted by the black tar road or
The tents of the Bedouin
Or the rest stop to quench the thirst

Captured Moments

Silently the road travels around
Upon or over the mountains,
The traveler can catch a glimpse
Of the circular stone dug-outs
Which stand alone upon the high peaks
Reminding all who pass below
Of a not-so-long-ago war
When this desert land was divided

The traveler cannot imagine
What was there here to fight for?
It was just a hot desert then
As the traveler knows it now!

Ellenelizabeth Cernek

Unobtainable?

Vacant, half-built villa
Stands looking upon
The harbor of
Mini Hashish

Standing incomplete
Watching years go by
Unlived in
Yet weather worn

Upon the cliff
      It watches the sea
Season after season
      Yet it's not for sale
For any reason

It stole my heart
      On first glance

All I want is to give it
      A lived-in chance
For it has no future
      With construction halted

Captured Moments

It's stolen my heart
And in possessing it
I cannot falter

Dreams of sitting upon its porch
      In shorts and a halter
Sipping mint tea
      And painting the sea

Setting my soul free

Ellenelizabeth Cernek

Mersa Matruh

Jingle, Jingle
Of the donkey-drawn taxi carriages

Dowah, Dowah
Of the cotton candy man

Psst, Psst
Of the salesmen boys along the beach

Swish, Swish
Of the aqua blue sea mingling with
The white, white powdered sands

Scuff, Scuff
Of the *ship-ships* hitting the sanded road

Moo or Bah
Of the loose herds crossing the streets

Flutter, Flutter
Of kites flying higher than the
Mosque's twin towers
The calling to worship
Five times a day echoing off the sea

I listen to Mersa Matruh
        As she asks me where I've been

Captured Moments

My Heart Beckons

My heart beckons
For the sea breeze
Over the balcony
Through the green shutters
To touch my soul
Cleansing my heart
To breathe endless salt sea air
Awakening my spirit
To seek true pleasure
Of my Egyptian family and friends
To appreciate the heat
Of the African summer
To be quenched and caressed
Within the clean Mediterranean Sea
To walk upon the white powdered sands
Of an ancient time passed
Breathing in deeply the salt sea air
My heart beckons
To remain with what is known
African heat, white powdered sands
Pure salt seawater and cleansing salt sea air

Ellenelizabeth Cernek

Sophie's Window

Ten-foot green shutters
Grace the street's first-floor balcony.
A wash line emptied each night
Of the daily boy's wear.
The 26th of July Street
Is a 35-mile-long, 6-lane main drag
Which stretches in front of the sea.
Palm trees along the middle island rustle
As the traffic whizzes by.
The night air, filled with barbecue corn,
And salt sea freshness.
The trot of a horse-drawn carriage
Breaks the noisy people and taxi horns.
The sunsets and the people are now just a hum,
We sit upon the balcony late into the night
Emptying all thoughts,
Finding lost souls,
Connecting a love of femininity,

Captured Moments

Crying for our husband's fates,
Praising our children's accomplishments,
Opening to each other's heart's desires,
Fusing to the end of time.
As the night grows into dawn,
And the sun rises,
The fishermen in their boats
Silently begin their day
Rowing west, past the Sultan's castle,
Through the harbor,
Then disappear.

First appeared at The Rift, *1998.*

Ellenelizabeth Cernek

The Faces It Touches

The full harvest moon
Descends for the night is finished
It is 5:00 am and the dark silence
Before dawn is brisk
The air smells sweet and clean
Grand Canyon Village still sleeps
On the terrace I listen
To the darkness
An owl hoots
Bidding all a good night
As the darkness turns into gray
The deer grazing begin to leave

We take the shuttle bus to
Yavapai Point joining the other tourists
The gray of a new day dawns
Changing into violet, then brilliant pinks
To oranges, and to yellows
The light plays on the Canyon
Changing its face
As the seconds stand still
The tourists, I among them
Watch in silent awe
As the Canyon is awakened by dawn
The hush over the crowd is incredible
Only broken by the sounds
Of the camera's shutter
Trying to catch the sunrise
As it changes the faces it touches

Captured Moments

Gypsy Road

Before me is my caravan
And we walk many miles
Before we are to camp
Each night our campfire
Is dug within a new site

We travel in a continuous motion
And dance to violins and tambourines
As the firelight casts a comforting glow

We follow our Gypsy Prince
To many new worlds
Where the locals always chase us
Requesting us to leave directly

We have no homes, only what we can carry
To call our own
To the gypsy the road is home

Living off the land
And at times the sleight of hand

Again before me is my caravan
With crying violins
The jingles of the rhythmic tambourines
As we the true vagabonds
Make our way upon
The Gypsy Road

First appeared at: http://www.aquillrelle.com/grouppoetryw.pdf.

Magic Alive

Captured Moments

Hunter Mountain

We drove over an hour
Before we even knew where we were going.
At last we ended up taking a hike.
We walked through snow up to our waists,
So white and pure, no footsteps walked before us,
Through trees that glistened from sunlight
Dancing upon the snow. We were silent
In the brisk air with the warmth of the sun upon us.
We walked to the edge of a frozen stream
And came upon an opening
Among the sentry of trees that guarded
A cliff frozen in time. Hearing water gurgling
The cylinder rose, frozen in mineral pastel hues,
A waterfall, frozen forever in time and our minds.
Silently viewing the treasure God bestowed upon us
No one dared to breathe or speak for fear Mother Nature
Would take away this sight.
With a glance at each other
We slowly returned within our own footsteps
In awe and silent meditation over what had gracefully
Touched our souls.
Only inside the car did I learn the name,
Kaaterskill Falls, a local told me.
But I thought it was a gift from Mother Nature
That God gave my heart and soul
Knowing it would stay with me forever.

Ellenelizabeth Cernek

Watchwoman

I have sat upon
Kaaterskill Falls
For a millennium

My arms searching
Reaching skyward
My roots spreading.

I have become a gazer
Standing testament
To long time spent.

I have witnessed
The inhales and exhales
Of countless days.

I have witnessed
Mankind's brilliance
In fortitude and defeat.

I am the original
Birch Tree who
Extends her reach.

I am now a grove
Of birch trees
Canopying the falls.

Captured Moments

I am the sentry
Watchwoman of Earth
Anticipating my rebirth.

In the quiets of
A winter storm
You may hear me:

"I open to the North,
I open to the East,
I open to the South,
I open to the West,
Elements complete my circle."

I stand and wait
Bare and naked
In winter's storms

For the coming
For my resurrection
For mankind to understand

Peace.

First appeared at: http://new.neopoet.com/node/648.

Ellenelizabeth Cernek

Shahenda

She stood on top of the crested falls
As sunlight danced within rushing waters,
Hands spread upward in meditation,
Exhorting the inner powers to appear.
Her full-length emerald green cloak
Whipping in the wind that burst forth,
Transfixed upon Kaaterskill Falls,
As the wind gushed, throwing her hood aside
Unleashing a wave of waist-length auburn hair.
Green eyes flashed as she chanted,
Dazzling rays of prism light
Danced forth from her right hip,
Her powers, being flocked together,
Echoing her words in the wind:
"I open to the North, I open to the East,
I open to the South, I open to the West;
Elements complete my circle!"
Suddenly, an awesome thunderclap,
Rain pelted the entire world,
The wind growled echoes within the ears.
All light was now turning into the shadows of evil,
As she had predicted, the dark times had begun.

Captured Moments

Her cloak whipped skyward
Standing straight above her upspread hands and head.
Her eyes cast up, her hair flung in the wind,
Her white gown blasted by speckles of black dirt,
Prism rays of color danced within her protected circle,
Illuminating the crest she stood upon, as she chanted.
Night swallowed day as darkness engulfed all.
There was nothing but silence, within those dark hours,
Broken only by dawn's awakening.
Soft cooing of birds filled the air,
The wind sighed gently, animals stirred cautiously.
Upon the crest of Kaaterskill Falls,
within the illuminating circle,
Stood a graceful tree, with emerald green leaves
In an upswept reach and a white spotted trunk.
Shahenda the wizard was seen no more.

First appeared at: http://archive.neopoet.com/forum/9004.

Ellenelizabeth Cernek

Creation of Shahenda

I am partly the moon
From the radiance of the sun

I am partly the earth
From the quenching of the rains

I am partly the sun
From the gravitation of the galaxy

I am partly the mountains
From the fire within

I am partly the water
From the winds of the atmosphere

I am partly green
From the photosynthesis of light

I am partly the daughter
From a father unknown

I am partly the sister
From siblings of others

Captured Moments

I am partly the maid
From the needs of the gaggle

I am partly the chef
From preparing diversity in life

I am partly the painter
From the scenes that haunt me

I am partly a palette
From the combination of hues

I am partly the word
From the poetry I weave

I am partly myself
From the world around me

First appeared at: http://new.neopoet.com/node/683.

Ellenelizabeth Cernek

Shahenda's Vocation

She steps onto the balcony, gazing
Far unto the edges of her realm.
Moonlight radiates strands of auburn hair
Spilling from beneath her night bonnet.

The night is young as she.
What wanting and needing
Stirs within her about him
Knowing not whence he came.

Gently a cool breeze brushes her cheek
She closes her eyes and cocks her head
Leaning on a palm which is not there.
Eyes slit open and she sees her lover.
She inhales and smells him
Opening her mouth, tasting him
Like a snake would sense its prey.

The wind blows the echo
Of his whisper
Knowing not of her loneliness
As she stands witness to mankind.

Captured Moments

She was born with purpose
Loving all upon earth
Caretaker of this world.

Duty and honor, her birthrights,
Chastity and solitude, her faith,
No man shall have her,
Born Shahenda,
Queen of queens,
The watchwoman of time,
The last wizard.

First appeared at: http://new.neopoet.com/node/627.

Ellenelizabeth Cernek

Blue

Sister through the window
Sits beside a heated hearth
Listening as the whispers of the moon
Fill her dreamy heart.

Foretelling winter's colored waters
Turning green lakes black with fever.

Where easy Star Mountain queen plops
What Thunder friend's heart aches?

As White-Ghost garden glows
In summer's crackling heat,
Bubbles silently, sparkles away.
For women bite far into the sky
Always mirroring, the blue clouds
Are only whispers of the moon
Answers to the sky?

Captured Moments

Travel far into the wind
Echoing the self
Into the candied forest,
Where the Mystical Love Monkey
Thunder, Star Mountain Queen,
And White-Ghost of the glowing garden
See all
As the whispering moon travels
Bringing forth
Morning Star,
                Causing blue skies blue
                      Blue.

First appeared at: http://www.helium.com/items/311908-poetry-the-sky.

Path's End

Where is the yellow brick road
That's in a child's dream?
Where is the line between
Morals taught and lessons learned?
Where is the blue horizon
Just as the storm arrives?
Where is the starry night sky
Just as dawn's born?
Where is the gingerbread house,
That's in fairy tale land?
Where is the dream of forever
That's at the path's end?

Captured Moments

Ellenelizabeth Cernek is a Sedona, AZ resident who enjoys art in all forms. Her sixth-grade teacher gave an assignment to write a poem. After she read Ellenelizabeth's first poem, the teacher gave her a blank book and a new pen, and told her to never stop writing.

In addition to being a writer, Ellenelizabeth is also a painter and photographer. She works in oil, acrylic, and watercolors. She has shown her art along the boardwalk of Wildwood, NJ, where she received honorable mention at the age of nine, and at The Cathedral Arts Festival sponsored by Grace Church in Jersey City, NJ. She loves to combine her art forms .

An avid traveler, Ellenelizabeth writes about the places, cultures, and people that have touched her life. Her work reflects different dimensions of space and culture she has absorbed in her travels.

Ellenelizabeth's work has been published in *The Rift*, *Wings Literary Magazine*, and several online poetry sites. This is her first collection.

www.ingramcontent.com/pod-product-compliance
Lightning Source LLC
Chambersburg PA
CBHW071737090426
42738CB00011B/2506